THE VOICE OF GOD

Dearest Patricia,
Be blessed
as you read.
Love,
Veronica

THE VOICE OF GOD

Veroncia Striggles

iUniverse, Inc.

New York Lincoln Shanghai

THE VOICE OF GOD

iUniverse books may be ordered through booksellers or by contacting:

iUniverse
2021 Pine Lake Road, Suite 100
Lincoln, NE 68512
www.iuniverse.com
1-800-Authors (1-800-288-4677)

Cover design by David Greenway

ISBN: 0-595-33865-8

Printed in the United States of America

This book is dedicated to the memory of our son
James Edward Striggles II.

We still miss you my darling………

Love Mom

SPECIAL DEDICATIONS

To: my "ever so precious" husband, James Striggles who pushed and pulled until I began to put my notes and thoughts in some resemblance of order. Because of you My Darling...I was able to stick to writing this book.

My darling children, Anthony (Tony), Algie (Al), and Rebecca (Becky).

Our lovely Alisa Marie, you have brought so much joy to our lives. I only pray that this book will give you comfort and strength to go on. "Pop" and I love you so much.

David Smith with open arms and loving hearts we welcome you into our family.

And my dear friend, Dion Mason, a prophet and man of God who knew just what to say to me when I started feeling like giving up and putting this book in a drawer. You always knew just when to call me. God bless you my friend.

SPECIAL THANKS TO

Pastor Kevin Vinson, Sr., you gave my book its title. After I finished teaching an extremely scaled down version of this book in bible study, you told the class that "THIS IS THE VOICE OF GOD." You also thanked me for sharing my experience with our congregation.

Renita Mitchell, you first tried to decipher my handwriting. Thank you for the hours that you spent typing the first part of this project.

A Special thanks to Antoinette Evans who worked so tirelessly typing and adding and deleting and editing each week. "Nette" you always had a smile and you never complained of being tired. I give you thanks and I declare that God's richest blessings are yours because you helped to give life to the things that God spoke to me. I Love You.

Dara Abston is studying to become an elementary educator. She caught every error in wording, spelling and pronunciation. Thank you.

My sweet cousin Sheila Watson, you stood silently by and allowed me to vent and unravel and then turn around and laugh. You seemed to be tuned into me when I needed a shoulder. We are real Buddies. Thank you for just listening.

Anyone struggling under the burden of grief due to a loss SHALL find comfort and encouragement within the covers of this book.

—God bless you as you read,
Veroncia Striggles

Contents

Introduction xvii

Foreword. xix

About the Author xxi

The Book xxv

The Voice of God 1

- *I Am Love* *3*
  - *Peace* *3*
  - *Joy* *4*
  - *Light* *4*
  - *Meek* *5*
  - *Salvation* *5*
  - *Life* *5*
  - *Glory* *7*
  - *Righteousness* *7*
  - *Holy* *7*
  - *Temperance* *8*
  - *Master Builder* *9*
  - *Refiner* *9*
  - *Problem Solver* *11*
  - *Preserver* *11*
  - *Focused* *12*
  - *Of Standard* *12*
  - *Progressive* *16*
  - *Rich* *18*

- *Faithful.* *18*
- *Truth* *20*
- *Rescue* *21*
- *Shelter.* *22*
- *The Door* *22*
- *Hope.* *23*
- *Healer.* *23*
- *Deliverance* *24*
- *Savior.* *24*
- *Restoration* *24*
- *Covenant Keeper* *25*
- *Authority.* *26*
- *Sufficiency.* *28*
- *Compassion* *28*
- *Investment.* *28*
- *Provider* *29*
- *Just* *29*
- *Judgment* *30*
- *Mercy* *30*
- *Teacher.* *31*
- *Wisdom.* *32*
- *Honor.* *32*
- *Friend.* *33*
- *Living Water.* *35*
- *Abundance* *35*
- *Sovereign.* *36*

I Am Alpha and Omega
Omnipotent
Omniscient
Omnipresent
Jehovah
Immutable

Call Me Tree of Life
    Hallowed
    Wonderful
    Excellent
    Jehovah Rapha
    Jehovah Shama
    Jehovah Jireh
    Jehovah Nissi
    Jehovah Shalom
    Rose of Sharon
I Am Strength
    Hedge of Protection
    Mathematician
    Choreographer
    Poet
Call Me Abba Father
I Am Greatest Artists
    Dunamis

Conclusion 43

INTRODUCTION

All scripture references and quotations taken from the King James Version of the Holy Bible. Study references taken from the New Strong's Exhaustive Concordance of the Bible. Personal names used with permission of owners.

FOREWORD

After a lifetime of Christianity and religious service, Veroncia Striggles has reached a maturity in Christ that allows her to see the goodness of the Lord in the midst of very turbulent times. We all struggle to make sense out of what seems senseless, unbelievable and unexplainable. Likewise, the sudden loss of her son raised many questions regarding her status in the Lord. And to each of us, there will come a time when our faith is challenged and stretched to its maximum limit. It is at this time that we must sensitize our ears to God's *"still small voice."*

We pray that Veroncia's book, *"The Voice Of God"* will bless you to hear that which is only audible through the spirit realm. There is so great a multitude of blessings in God's voice and to those who have an ear to hear; victorious living can be achieved. Take your time in reading and meditation of the contents within and allow your spirit to grow stronger in the Lord, ever trusting Him in every situation of life.

Bishop Charles H. Ellis III
Sr. Pastor, Greater Grace Temple
Assistant Presiding Bishop, PAW, Inc.

ABOUT THE AUTHOR

On October 8, 1946, I was the second of eleven children born to Christian parents. Sarah and Algie Evans were loving parents. With each new addition to our family, they felt their lives were the richer because of the newborn. We were raised to be strict Pentecostal/Apostolics. I thank God for Holy parents who trained us well.

Along the way, many things that were labeled sin at my church, I have learned through much study, are not sin. Many of those things however **are** weights that can hinder ones spiritual growth.

At the age of ten I responded to the Voice of God and was filled with the Holy Ghost. This was the beginning of my walk with God. God has always been my love. I love His word and His lifestyle. However, as a child (both naturally and spiritually) I thought and acted as a child. It was in my mid teens that I recognized the Voice of God through my dreams. I later realized that they were sometimes Prophetic. I recognized the Voice of God and learned the value of the gift that I have living and working in me. Some of my dreams I shared with my mother, who was truly a virtuous woman of God. Other dreams and visions I kept to myself.

The years passed, and as they did, I sought a closer and more intimate knowledge of God. As I grew in Him and learned to crucify the deeds of my flesh; He showed Himself more in my life. I became comfortable in my walk with God and I truly love Him.

In May of 1965, I met a young man, James Edward Striggles. In January 1966, we began talking seriously. In May of that year James was drafted to serve in the United States Army, during the Vietnam Era. During the two years of our separation, we engaged the postal service as our means of daily contact. My darling James returned home in May of 1968. We were married on October 12,1968. To date, we have been married 35 wonderful years.

We were blessed with four children, three sons and one daughter. James II was born tens months after we were married. He was our delight. James was very smart and lovable. He was so smart that he was fully potty trained at seven months old. In January 1971, our second child was born. Anthony was more lovable than James the Second (if that is possible). However, Anthony was "ALL BOY." In dealing with and raising our sons, it was like the fairy-tale of Snow White and Rose Red. They were total opposites, but we loved them and enjoyed watching them grow.

While they were yet sitting on my lap, their father and I taught them about God and His never ending love. We also tried to impress upon them His requirements of us.

Two and one half years after Anthony, baby number three was on his way. I knew the gender of the baby because I saw him in a dream. I had prayed so hard for a little girl, but I was overjoyed when I was able to hold Algie, our third son. For the next ten years we were happy raising our three sons. They were very active in our church, good in school, and dedicated to the family structure. God really blessed us in that our sons were water baptized and Holy Ghost filled at a very young age.

Two months before our last child was born, a pretty little girl, (June 24, 1984), my mother went home to be with the Lord. However, two weeks before her passing, which was on April 12, 1984, Sarah named our daughter...Rebecca. Rebecca has been our realization of all that is soft, sweet, lovely, and feminine. After the birth of Rebecca I was almost totally bedridden, she was a high-risk pregnancy. The pregnancy and mourning the loss of my mother sent my immune system into a downward spiral. We did not know that I was carrying the dormant rheumatoid disease gene. My doctors thought I had leukemia. Also in the span of three years I had serious pneumonia three times.

I grew weary of the pain, and not being able to do for myself or my family. I could not enjoy my position as wife and mother, and so I prayed to die. I resigned myself to the idea that my loving husband and darling children would fare better with a healthy wife and mom. One Sunday I had an open eye vision. I saw first my husband on a long road, shoulders drooped and head hung down. He was walking all alone. I sat up to get a better look, and when I did, I saw my daughter on a blanket in a corner all alone. I prayed and pleaded with God to heal and restore me. There were many hard days and nights to follow but I refused to let go. When I seemed at my lowest, God's angels would appear in my room and sing to me. God was faithful concerning His promises to me, and today I walk with Him enjoying the benefits of his Divine Word, "By His stripes I was healed."

For more information or comments,

Write to:
Veroncia Striggles
23601 Gardner
Oak Park, Michigan 48237-2470
            Or
Email: jamesnronnie@yahoo.com

THE BOOK

Many songs, poems, books, and plays are born as a result of some life changing event. This writing is one such "Baby." In the almost sixteen years that I had been married, my mother had been my prayer partner, confidant, and the one to keep me encouraged. For the next three years after her death, I felt so alone. I went through a time that seemed as though it would be my end. However, God was still faithful. When seemingly I was at my lowest, God sent ministering angels to a corner of my bedroom. I had never heard, nor have I heard since, the beautiful melodies that were ministered to me. Sometimes I would call my oldest son (James) into the bedroom to see if he could hear what I was hearing. His answer was always the same…"Mom, it's the fever talking." At those times I would drift into a most peaceful sleep and awake hours later feeling refreshed.

At the end of three years and much prayer, God began to strengthen me. I had lost so much weight. I had lost down to 73 pounds before I started gaining weight again. I began to go out with my family more often. At this point I must add that my father, sisters, and older cousin helped my husband in our home. My father would visit Rebecca and I during the day. My sisters transported our sons to school and cleaned our house. My aunt would make delicious Chicken Fricasee to help increase my appetite. My cousin Janice, a nurse at one of the major hospitals in Detroit, would come and give her medical advice. The praying women of our church, made weekly visits to pray, minister and encourage our hearts. My pastor's wife, LaVern Staten, kept the cards of comfort coming through the mail. There were two other very important people that gave assistance during this time, Dorothy Jean Knight and Alexander Vaught, Sr. They also kept the little "special dishes" coming to help me regain my appetite.

My darling husband was always there, loving, praying, and watching over me. Initially it seemed as though he was watching me slip away. One Saturday night I almost did. But, because of the prayers of so many of God's people especially our pastor, Bishop Gaston Staten, my sister Donna, my sons and husband, I'm still here. That night, I told my enemy, the devil, that his attacks against me were over. God honored my declaration and faith in Him, and He has restored me.

From my bedside and easy chair, I watched our daughter grow. All too soon she started kindergarten. However, I was blessed to drive her to and from school when the time came for her to attend kindergarten.

The years and months passed, God continued to speak to me. Through those years, I studied God's Word with a fervor that amazed even me. I didn't realize at the time that God was preparing me. As I studied His Word, God continued to speak to me in dreams and visions. Many times the night would find me in my living room, praying and weeping before the Lord. Sometimes, I had tears of joy and other times I had tears because of the things I did not understand. My scratch pads would run out of paper because of the volume of information God imparted to me. My love for Him grew. He knew me and I was more and more familiar with His Voice, and I loved Him more.

In his mid teens, our son, James II, acknowledged and accepted his call to the ministry. Before this, God had anointed him as a gifted artist, writer, musician, composer and singer. In September of 1995, James married a Godly young woman, Alisa Anderson. Theirs was a storybook marriage. It was God Anointed and Appointed in all ways. One year after marriage, James and Alisa started Prevailing Word Church. James' brothers, Anthony and Algie became members of their church. There were many requests of the church members needing gray hairs. After we sought the Lord through fasting and prayer, God gave us a sign. My husband and I became members of Prevailing Word, and of course, so did our daughter Rebecca. As a stamp of His approval, of our obedience, God gave Rebecca the Holy Ghost on Easter Sunday morning 1998. With our pastors blessings we began worshipping and working at Prevailing Word Church.

The church grew and did various out reach ministries. We were overjoyed to see God use our children in such a powerful and spirit-filled way. Things felt so good, so right, and so spiritually prosperous. Many family members and friends became members of the Prevailing Word church. God sent in many new converts also.

In 1999, Pastors James and Alisa Striggles were blessed to visit Africa to minister. During their one and a half week stay Pastor James' system was invaded by some type of bacteria that affected his heart and kidneys. This caused him much pain and suffering. James lived through many sleepless nights. Pastor James became tired of the suffering and decided it was time for him to go home. He would say to us and the congregation that God had something better than this for him.

On January 30, 2003, I spoke with him for about 15 minutes shortly after 10 a.m. He had called to check on me because I was not at Bible Study the night before due to a cold. James sounded good and strong and was very happy. We ended our call because of a project he had to finish. The two people working with him on the project had arrived at his home. They were his brother Anthony and god-brother Earl Orr, Jr. Before hanging up James promised me, if possible, he would call back after the completion of his project. Before twelve noon James II, our first born son, and pastor, had gone on to be with the Lord. He had completed his project and then he apprehended "that better thing…" **"For to be absent from this body is to be present with the Lord…"** and this was much better than what he was going through.

There is no way I can describe the tailspin that the family, church, and friends experienced. I cannot speak for my husband, my daughter in-law, nor our remaining three children, but I was in the darkest tunnel of my life. Do you remember that I said that I was familiar with the Voice of God? Well, I could not feel Him and I definitely did not hear Him. For days, weeks, and months we were surrounded by the love of friends and family. They all tried to comfort and ease our pain in their own way. One comfort to the family was that Pastor James was Holy Ghost filled and that he did not suffer as he left us. He looked at Earl and gently said, **"It is finished."** He was gone from a body that had an enlarged and diseased heart that could not pump strong enough to keep him alive.

For many days and nights following I could only see blackness when I closed my eyes. Let me say, that I know now, that we cannot hold back the night…nor the darkness can we outrun. We cannot even rush the morning sunlight. But, be assured God will take us through our darkness. I know for a fact, born out of experience, that God was in that seemingly endless, dark tunnel with us every step of the way. After many nights of hurting and crying and wishing the phone would ring and wake me to hear our son's voice on the other end, I finally, truly, turned to the only source I knew, God. At times there would be knocks at the door that sounded like Pastor James' knock and my heart would almost stop beating.

In the midst of my darkness I asked God to show Himself again. I needed to experience His presence. In the midst of my pain He answered me saying, **"I AM."** I listened prayerfully for more. The Voice kept repeating **"I AM."** As the days and weeks went by, I saw, heard, and understood more, **"I AM THAT I AM."** With renewed fervor I thought to search the scripture. As I studied an attribute of God and exhausted all that I felt there was to know, He would gently whisper another of His attributes into my spiritual ear. The one scripture that kept coming to me is Exodus 3:10-14.

THE VOICE OF GOD

.........AND GOD SAID

"Come now therefore, and I will send thee unto Pharaoh, that thou mayest bring forth my people the children of Israel out of Egypt. And Moses said unto God, Who Am I that go unto Pharaoh, and that I should bring forth the children of Israel out of Egypt? And He (God) said, certainly I will be with thee; and this shall be a token unto thee, that I have sent thee: when thou hast brought forth the people out of Egypt, ye shall serve (Me) God upon this mountain. And Moses said unto God, Behold, when I come unto the children of Israel, and shall say unto them, The God of your fathers have sent me unto you; and they shall say unto me, What is His name? What shall I say unto them? And God said unto Moses, I AM THAT I AM: And He (God) said, Thus shall thou say unto the children of Israel, I AM hath sent me unto you." (KJV Exodus 3:10-14)

Moses knew God, but the majority of his kinsmen, the Isaelites, did not. This is why Moses questioned God as to how to present His plan of deliverance to his people.

You will find pages through-out this book labeled "My thoughts and notes." This page is for you to further add the Wonderful and Awesome attributes of our God. I know that I do not have it all contained here in my book. God speaks to us all. We only need to be still and hear Him.

I AM LOVE I AM

Love is the corner stone, the plumbline, and the anchor upon which all of God's commandments are based and settled. God said, "If you love Me you will keep my commandments." In John 15:12 Jesus says, "This is My commandment, that you love one another, as I have loved you." God and His son Jesus are one and Jesus was telling us one of Gods main and foremost attributes or characteristics. I AM Love. In Romans 5:5, "The love of God is shed abroad in our hearts by the Holy Ghost." In the Songs of Solomon when the writer is speaking to His love, He says, "I cover thee with love because I AM." The book of Ephesians chapters five and six instructs the husband, wife, children, masters and servants how to love. "It is My love for you that caused Me to step back when My Son was crucified to bring you back into My arms. You will know, and the world will know, that you have My love, by the way you forgive and love one another. I, LOVE, will not let you speak ill of your fellow man. I, LOVE, will give you the heart to go that extra mile when you know you have already gone as far as is necessary. Love (ME) will cause you to love your neighbor as yourself," (Galatians 5:14). Paul prayed that the love of the saints would abound more and more in knowledge and in all judgment, (Phillipians 1:9). My love covers your multitude of sin and inequities. They are so covered that I remembered them no more. My love will cast your transgressions into the sea of forgetfulness. I AM LOVE I AM, and the only true lover of your soul.

I AM PEACE I AM

"Peace I leave with you, My peace I give unto you not as the world giveth, give I unto you," (St. John 14:27). In Psalms 4:8 David said, "I will lay down and sleep in peace because you make me safe." He is saying I have peace in my spirit. There is peace where ever the Son of Peace is. Psalms 34:14 tells us to "Seek peace and pursue it." **When you seek peace you are looking for Me because I AM Peace, I AM. My peace passes all understanding and all human comprehension.** Philippians 4:7 states, "And the peace of God, which passeth all understanding, shall keep your heart and minds through Christ Jesus." **In your darkest midnight and in your saddest season and in times of despair, meditate on ME. I Am that peace in your mind. I, PEACE, will keep your heart, mind and spirit. My peace is so secure that the world cannot take it** from you. No situation or harm can destroy the peace that I give. Keep your heart and mind stayed on ME and I will keep you in perfect peace because I AM PEACE I AM.

I AM JOY I AM

"Therefore with joy shall you draw water out the wells of salvation," (Isaiah 12:3). I Am that water, that Joy. My joy flows as a well of water. I am that Joy that causes you to want to draw from ME. In John 16:22, the joy that I give, no man can take from you. I Am Joy, a joy that the world cannot destroy because the world cannot destroy ME. I Am your song of praise and joy. In your darkest night because I Am Joy within you, you will be able to endure until the morning light appears. I Am bells of joy ringing in your soul. I AM JOY I AM. I make you glad (to have joy) through my word. My works are great and my thoughts for you are deep, (Psalms 92).

I AM LIGHT I AM

In Psalms 27:1, David is singing a song of declaration that I Am his Light. 1 John 1:5 states that "I Am light and in me there is no darkness at all." According to Matthew 5:14 because of ME you are the beacon of salvation for your fellow man. As I Am the Light in you, so should you also be light in the world. I Am the Light in you that all men see in this sin darkened society. In the beginning, before your time was, I called forth light. I have never stopped that light. In the beginning also was the word which was made flesh. This flesh walked in the Light of ME. Let this Light be a lamp to your footsteps and a light to your path as you walk in this world today. In Christ Jesus, I Am the True Light. I Am that light in you shining as a city set upon a hill. Philippians 2:15 says it best, "That ye may be blameless and harmless, the sons of God, without rebuke, in the midst of a crooked and perverse nation, among whom ye shine as lights in the world." I Am that Light I Am. When those walking in the shadow of sin look at you, they should see ME in you. Show them the way to ME by your fellowship with ME. I AM LIGHT (for today) I AM.

I AM MEEK I AM

Psalms 149:4 says that the Lord taketh pleasure in His people; He will beautify the meek with salvation. Psalms 25:9 states God is so pleased with the meek that He will guide us in judgment ; and the meek will He teach His way. **My Meek One's are teachable and I, God, delight in teaching them my way. I Am that beautiful salvation of the Meek. Also, and again, the Meek will not speak evil of his brother or sister. There is no guile found in the mouth of the meek. The Meek speak what is lovely, right, pure, true, and of a good report. The meek are not weaklings, but they will step aside rather than seek their own rights. My Meek Ones know that I will elevate them in their day. My character (spirit) of Meekness within my children gives them the strength to stand still and see My salvation. I AM MEEK I AM.**

I AM SALVATION I AM

You will find in Exodus 15:2 that Moses is singing a song about ME, (God). He sang that I Am his strength and salvation. In Psalms 24:1 David sang praises unto ME…"The Lord is my light and my salvation." I Am your only salvation. Some trust in horses, (cars), riches, (jobs, stock markets or inheritances) and strength (physical and mental). **I Am true salvation for the world today. All of these other things will fail, run out, pass away or bankrupt, but I Am strong and live forever. I save from sin and preserve you until the more perfect day. I Am salvation for your life. When all about you seems topsy-turvy just stand still and see ME…your Salvation. I save upright in an upside down world. In Isaiah 62:1, I will be as a Lamp Of Salvation that burns bright. I Am Salvation for my people.** Psalms 62:6-7 states "He only is my rock and my salvation; He is my defence;; I shall not be moved. In God is my salvation and my glory: The rock of my strength, and my refuge is in God." **I AM that SALVATION I AM.**

I AM LIFE I AM

In the book of Deuteronomy 30:19 you will find, "I call heaven and earth to record this day against you," that is, the day that you hear my voice. "Today I have set before you life and death, blessings and cursing. Therefore (I sug-

gest) choose life, (ME) that both thou and thy seed may live." When you choose ME/LIFE you save yourself, and your family, or household. There is nothing so beautiful as generation after generation walking with the Lord. Just because decades ago someone chose to walk this Christian Way, I am saved today. Our daughter, Rebecca, is a fifth generation in holiness. My great-grandmother chose a life of holiness and therefore, blessing through her obedience to God's call. St. John 11:25, bears out Deuteronomy 30:19, that I Am the eternal LIFE which is promised to them that believe and obey. This earth is not our final home. There is life after death. In that day when Jesus comes to take us to God's heaven we must have within us the power of God that will bring our dead bodies to life. Those that are alive and remain on this earth must have the same spirit that Jesus has in him to energize us for the flight to heaven.

We may feel that we are very much alive. We often are blessed with benefits that cause us to feel that we are living the high or the good life. However, we have not begun to live until we make God the seat of our joy and the heart of our contentment. No matter how good it all may seem, unless we acknowledge that life is nothing without God, the good times are empty. In this world's system, people strive to climb higher. We strive for bigger, better and more and yet, we are not satisfied. This is because we have not permitted God to be a part of it all. Jesus said, "I am the true vine. I am in my father God." I see us as drowning souls. God sends the rescuer. Because we think we know what is best, we fight. In the natural, if a drowning person fights his rescuer, they both perish.

We don't know the way that we should take. Jesus came to rescue us. We have to let him guide us to safety. We cannot feel that our knowledge will do anything other than cause us to drown in life's rivers of care and disappointments and sin. God in Christ Jesus is our hope of Life. Choose Him and live. God alone satisfies. Life is worthless without Him. Let God in and find abundant life no matter what your status in society. God said, I AM LIFE I AM." Find me in Psalms 16:11...David wrote, "That I will show you the Path Of Life and in my presence is fullness of joy." Also at my right hand are pleasures forevermore. I Am Life. Those who do not choose God will also live eternally but not in His glory. Choose ME...LIFE and live. I AM LIFE I AM.

I AM GLORY I AM

Psalms 84:11 states, **I Am that glorious attribute that exalts you before men. I Am that light of glory that caused the soldiers to fall away as dead men when they approached My Son to arrest Him and to do Him harm. I Am the Glory that sustained Him just before His death on the cross. When you live holy and walk upright before ME, I glory in giving you all of the good things that you seek. I will cause you to prosper and to be in health even as your soul prospers in ME. When you prosper spiritually, I Am glorified. I Am glorified when you are filled with righteousness and praise. In Exodus 33, Moses has pleased Me, and he has found grace in My sight. Moses asked that I show him My glory. Not only did I do that, but I also showed him goodness and mercy. In My excellence, I show forth Glory. I give Glory to My righteous ones. I AM GLORY I AM.**

I AM RIGHTEOUSNESS I AM

Righteous, yes, this is I. Psalms 11:7 calls me righteous and this account declares that I love righteousness, my eye and my face, is ever turned to my Righteous Ones. Also Matthew 5:6, lets you know when you desire and seek ME (GOD) I will fill you up with Me…I Am Righteousness. I look at my image (you) and I behold you adorned in Me, (My Image) which is righteousness. When I am in you and you are in Me, I cause you to flourish as a palm tree and to be rooted like the cedars of Labanon. When you are planted in me, My Righteousness causes you always to flourish in My presence. I Am Righteousness I Am. I cause you to bring forth fresh righteous fruits no matter how old you become as you walk in My righteousness. In ancient of days, you are more securely anchored and more fruitful in Righteousness. Your roots in Me never rot and are never plucked up, because I AM in you as the root of Righteousness…I AM.

I AM HOLY I AM

In Leviticus 19:2, I spoke to Moses and told him to declare unto Israel…"Ye shall be holy: for I the Lord your God am holy." Yes I AM HOLY. I require holy people in my likeness and my image. I cannot operate or walk contrary

to Myself. You can walk perfect before Me because I AM. And with Me in you, you can be holy. Without holiness it is impossible to please Me. To live for Me means that you will operate totally opposite of what others think, do and feel. Your walk with Me will not be easy, but My grace for you is sufficient to keep you. Remember, to be Holy will cost you. In My word you will find that the Godly (Holy) shall suffer persecution. Without holiness no man will see Me. I Am Holy, seek My face, (My presence). Be clean "having your garments of righteousness free from spots, wrinkles, blemishes, or any such thing." Ephesians 1:3-4 spells it out best, "Blessed be the God and father of our Lord Jesus Christ, who hath blessed us with all spiritual blessings in heavenly places in Christ: according as He hath chosen us in Him before the foundation of the world, that we should be holy and without blame before Him in love." Gods plan for us from the beginning, our destiny, requires that we live holy. **You can live holy because I, AM HOLY, I AM.**

I AM TEMPERANCE I AM

Galations 5:22-26 says, "But the fruit of the spirit is love, joy, peace, longsuffering, gentleness, goodness, faith, meekness, temperance: against such there is no law. And they that are Christ's have crucified the flesh with the affections and lusts. If we live in the Spirit, let us walk in the Spirit. Let us not be desirous of vain glory, provoking one another, envying one another." **When you walk according to these, My attributes of the spirit filled, you will not and cannot go off center. I AM control, that causes you to discipline yourselves to line up with My word and commandments. With temperance, you can live a consistently, holy life. You will not be too holy to seek more and more of Me. Yet you will not be so sloughful that you will sit down and be content with your two or three scriptures that you have committed to memory.** We are created free-will creatures. God gives us the ability to control our will by His power. **The steps of a good man are ordered by ME. Let ME control your life. I AM temperance. I AM self-control. I keep you so that you will not fall into satan's snares. In order to maintain self-control, "lay aside every weight (little no harm things) and the sin that does so easily beset (control) you and run with patience this race that is before you." Let Me temper you so that you never falter nor fail. I AM TEMPERANCE I AM.**

I AM MASTERBUILDER I AM

You are fearfully and wonderfully made. I do not dwell in places of brick and mortor. I live in you. You are a chosen vessel. You are a royal priesthood. You are my temple. You are my habitation. You are my manifested blueprint before the foundation of the world. I chose you before time. I knew you while you were yet in your mother's belly. I have made all of you (humanity) to be fittly joined together in Me. Daily you are growing into a holy temple…you (all of humanity) are being built together for a dwelling place for Me in your heart and spirit, (Ephesians 2:21-22). I Am still making you. I see you becoming a perfect masterpiece in Me. Yield your body to be shaped and molded and constructed by My word. You are destined to be a perfected soul in ME because I AM (your) MASTERBUIDER I AM.

I AM REFINER I AM

Isaiah 48:10-11 says, "Behold, I have refined thee, but not with silver; I have chosen thee in the furnace of affliction. For mine own sake, even for mine own sake, will I do it: for how should I let my name be polluted? **And I will not give my glory unto another." I see your rough state. I already know your end while you are still in the beginning. As you go through life's trials and afflictions, I purify and refine you. Let Me purify you. My fire of love will burn off all dross and impurities of your flesh-man. Watch Me cause you to be as pure as gold. Be as gold that has been through the refiner's fire. You will come forth as pure as gold. Pure gold is transparent. Through your transparency the world will see Me in you. I do not use the twelve, ten, nor seven steps down from sin to bring you to perfection. By My might and power you are perfected and refined. I will do this thing in you for My own sake and My own glory. I will not give My glory to another. You are made perfect only in Me. I AM REFINER I AM.**

MY THOUGHTS AND NOTES

I AM PROBLEM SOLVER I AM

Find in Psalms 119:130 that the very entrance of my word (into your heart) turns on the light of understanding. I cause you to see the answer, the way out, and the solution. David said, "I will lift my eyes to the hills from whence cometh my help" and all of "my help comes from the Lord," (Psalms 121:1-2). I AM in that high and holy place waiting for you to acknowledge ME, and I will solve your problems. David also said, "In my distress I cried and you delivered me." In Isaiah 43:16, I make a way in the sea and a path through the mighty waters. When the prophet, Elijah, asked Me to shut up heaven so there would be no rain, I did. When he was faced with the effects of the drought and famine, I solved his problem by sending him to I Kings 17:3-4,6…"Get thee hence, and turn thee eastward, and hide thyself by the brook Cherith, that is before Jordan. And it shall be, that thou shalt drink of the brook; and I have commanded the ravens to feed thee there. And the ravens brought him bread and flesh in the morning, and bread and the flesh in the evening; and he drank of the brook." For the Prophet, the problem is solved. Where there seemed to be no way, I made a way. I cause you to prosper. I give you good health, I give you the bright ideas and ways, so that your hands are able to get wealth. Your problems are solved even as you yield your soul to prosper in Me. I AM PROBLEM SOLVER I AM.

I AM PRESERVER I AM

I have made you the salt of the earth. I Am preservation living in you. As long as I Am in you, you are preserved until a more perfect day. David rejoiced in knowing My willingness and power to preserve. In Psalms 32:7, he said that I was his hiding place and the one to preserve him in trouble. In Psalms 41:2, I preserve and I keep alive them that consider and help the poor. I Am high above the earth and exalted above any situation or any god. In Psalms 97:9-10, for those that love Me and hate evil, those souls I preserve. I preserve the souls of My saints, and deliver them out of the hands of the wicked. I in you make you the salt of the earth. Your spice, in situations of life, tastes like ME. I Am wonderful and I change not. If you lose your ability to salt or to be preserved, you become good for nothing. I Am able to keep you because, I AM PRESERVER I AM.

I AM FOCUSED I AM

Hebrews 13:9 says that I Am the same yesterday, today, and forever. Let your heart be established and not carried away be every new phase or the latest and the hottest religious craze. It is a good thing to know ME and to rest in ME. James 1:17 says, "All good and perfect gifts come from Me, the father of lights…in Me, there is no variableness (wavering) neither shadow of turning." I Am about My business and I Am always the same. You will never find a hint (shadow) of change in Me. I know the plans that I have for you. Walk with me and stay close, because I will never leave you. It's a good thing to renew your vows to ME. I will at no time turn My back on a humble and contrite heart. I Am tuned into you because I AM FOCUSED I AM.

I AM OF STANDARD I AM

I am not welfare, but I desire that you fare well. I Am not a "Sugar Daddy," however, I give you the desires of your heart when your ways please ME. I Am vengeful and jealous. I hold all the cards in the game of life. I have already wooed and won you by giving my only begotten Son to die for your sins. I have paid a great price for you. This is why I can say that I have made the rules for this life. You have not chosen Me, but I have chosen you. I only ask that you love ME in return. Please do not offend Me by whoring after other loves. According to My word, there are more ways than one that you can exhibit spiritual whoredom and idol worship.

I Corinthians 6:20, states that you are bought with a price, therefore glorify (ME), GOD, in your body and in your spirit, which are Mine. There are several ways to commit spiritual whoredom. One is; Church Wise—sometimes we leave our places of worship, because of a roving lustful eye. We are desiring things at the "BIG CHURCH" across town. You like their choir and the way they make you dance during the worship services. Men, you think that the women there are so beautiful, and ladies, you say you are getting older and still have no husband. You feel that it is all right to go ahead and attend a dead, wordless and "miracle deficient" church. After mixing and mingling and after hooking yourself a mate, you return to your former place of worship. I, GOD, call that whoredom, because you have stepped outside of our covenant to fix your situation yourself. When you play the part of the harlot, Revelation 18:8 says

that you should be utterly burned with fire. I, GOD, will be the one judging your actions. Secondly, Spiritually, **I Corinthians 6:17 adds "He that is joined unto the Lord is one spirit." How then can you freely worship with, or condone, any worship that is not for ME.** You say "As long as I treat everybody right and fair, I'm all right and they're all right." You say, "I worship the true GOD," yet you condone others worship of Mohammed, Buddah, Hari Christna, Allah, and so on. It's their choice and this is a free country. You say you don't like to cause trouble. There is only one way to God. There is only one way to heaven. Anybody who tries to enter any other way, is a thief and a robber. We all know that heaven is a holy place, there is no sin there, not even a smart sinner. **I Am Standard, only those like ME and in my image will enter My Rest. I, God, said that your bodies are the temple of the holy ghost. Will you take your members that belong to Me and link them to a harlot? (I Corinthians 6:15). Do not commit spiritual fornication. A Third Way to commit spiritual whoredom is Idol worship; which is also against My standard. Revelation 17:1 calls this Idol Worshipper "A Great Whore." You make your job, your mate, your children and the luxuries that I have given, idols. You make them an idol when they come before worship of ME. When you pay tribute to statues, smoke signals, or any object, animate or inanimate, you defile your temple or (My dwelling place). I created heaven and earth and all that dwells there. Give the glory to Me.**

When I was a child, I knew of a man who owned (what at that time was) a luxury car. If it was raining, he would not go to church. If it started to rain during service, he would leave church to take his car home and put it in the garage. Also, as a young adult, I had a male friend that attended my church. He met and married a sweet young lady from another church. They were both holy ghost filled. This couple began their family the year after they were married. The husband had a good paying job. He loved his wife and children dearly. He tried to provide them with the best that his salary could afford. He bought some land and planned to build a nice big home for his ever increasing family. There is nothing wrong with any of this that I have mentioned. The error was in that he decided to do as much as possible of the work himself. So that he could keep working full time at his job and build a home, he had to put church attendance on hold. I was told that in order to be sure that he was not remiss in shepherding, the young man's pastor, one day, went to the building site to talk to him. The young man assured his pastor that he was doing well. He was still saved and planned to return to the house of God as soon as his home was finished. In Exodus 20:5,

I,(GOD), said "I the Lord thy God am a jealous God." You did not choose ME, I have chosen you, (St. John 15:16). The days, weeks and months slipped by. Two years passed before the house was finished. Somewhere in that span of time, this young man was introduced to drugs.

My friend, do you not know that we are never in limbo? We serve either God of heaven, Jehovah, or the god of this world, satan. By the time this young man's wife and children moved into their home, the husband/father was so strung out on drugs, that he never really was able to live with them. The last time that I can remember seeing him, he was sitting on the floor against the wall in the corridor of his church. He did not even know where he was. His idol worship took him to a place where, though we all loved him, we could not reach him. If I can give this story a moral, it is, give God His or He will take that that you owe Him and more. We can not decide that once we have supplied our loved ones needs, that we'll serve God. God supplies our needs and makes it possible for us to accomplish what we invision. We cannot afford to decide, once we have made it to the top of the corporate ladder, we'll worship God. We cannot put our Holy God in the passenger seat. He must lead and guide and direct us. A Fourth way; Unholy Communication is another aspect of whoredom. Spending too much time with non-believers. We cannot engage in "Missionary Dating" and expect this to be acceptable to God. How can two walk together, except they agree? Does your walk agree with the ways of God? Acts 15:20…"Abstain from pollution's of idols, and from fornication…" You say, "I'm just hanging with them or listening to the stories of my non-believing friends, because they lead such exciting lives. No, I don't do what they do, I just listen and watch." Acts 1:32 says, "They that commit such things (sin) are worthy of death, not only (them that) do the same, but those who have pleasure in them that do them.

We must also be careful of the movies we watch, the books we read, and the pictures that we enjoy oogling. We even have to be careful of the lyrics of the songs that we permit to enter our hearts and minds. I Corinthians 10:6 states we should not lust after evil things." I John 2:16 tells us that all that is in the world is the lust of the flesh, lust of the eyes and the pride of life. All of this is of the world and not of our Heavenly Father. Lust is nothing more than a strong and sometimes insatiable desire. We must be careful that our desires are Godlike. Be careful also of a Fifth way; Leisure Time—Do we visit the sick? Do we call shut ins? Do we care for widows and the fatherless that we know about? **When you sacrifice of yourself and your time and your substance you exhibit My love** attribute. **Make these things a part of your worship of ME.** "Pure religion **and undefiled religion before (ME), GOD, is this...to visit the fatherless and the widows in their affliction, and to keep yourselves unspotted from the world,"** (James 1:27). Also I Thessalonians 5:22 God's likeness includes abstaining from all appearance of evil. **I, God, rested from all my labour after creation of you and the wondrous things of nature that you enjoy even today. So you see, I Am not against leisure, but do not let it come between you and I. Keep your mind stayed on me and I'll keep you in perfect peace, and you will have rest for your soul. This is My Standard of life for you.**

As I write this, I want to include **MY OWN OPINION** of idol worship. I am very careful about our National Anthem and Pledge of Allegiance to our flag. I am very patriotic, and I am aware of our instructions as Christians, to obey the laws of our land/country. In so many places in our nation, prayer is taken out of schools. Pictures of Jesus, the ten commandments, and nativity scenes on public property are all outlawed by the courts in most states. However, in every place of education or government, we see the United States flag and statements or inscriptions "God Bless America." God is asking, **How can I bless when you as a people try to hide Me? Raise your children to know God and to pledge to live holy even if this nation decides to do otherwise.** Many of us salute the flag, but do not know how to really respect what it stands for. The Founding Fathers of our nation built and established our government on the bible and the holy laws of God. If we understand the Ten Commandments, then we have learned what God has said that we shall not do. And we can live in safety. In addition, while saluting the flag, we must be careful that it does not become a symbol of worship. We must Pledge Allegiance to all that is right. However, we cannot support all "rights." Our allegiance to uphold the law, as set forth by our courts cannot jeopardize our allegiance of holy and righteous integrity.

I, God, admonish you, as my bride, you cannot wear my garment of righteousness into the nightclub, nor the casino or such places. Personally, I have heard about the luscious buffets that are in the casinos. But, if I search hard enough I will find the same delicacies elsewhere. **Although I judge the heart of mankind, I expect the outer man to portray what is in your heart. Dress as is becoming holiness. Do not send mixed messages to your fellow man. You say you belong to ME, do not let your attire say something totally different as men and women of GOD. You are a peculiar people, you have been chosen by ME. Do not defile my temple with illicit love affairs, whether they be**

spiritual or the flesh. Exodus 20:7 says, "Do not take my name in vain." Don't say that you represent ME and do not walk the walk, talk the talk, or live the life of Godliness. Do not permit your life's "busyness" or social climbing to come between you and I. I Am a "Jealous Lover." Psalms 78:56-59 speaks about Israel provoking ME to jealousy and anger. With their idol worship, they forsook our love covenant and "I Hated Israel for this." I Am of Standard therefore walk before me and be perfect. Also, do not let your secular education supersede your quest to know more about ME spiritually. I AM STANDARD OF I AM.

I AM PROGRESSIVE I AM

No one and nothing stays the same. I am not in limbo and neither will you ever be. Only one time in history has it (seemed) that things stood still. In the wilderness my children stayed for forty years. I was waiting for them to turn their hearts to ME. Even then they were not in limbo, they continued to circle the wilderness of Kadesh for forty years, always moving in their own unrighteousness. When you learn Me, you will understand even more so that I am ever progressive. Phillipians 4:13-14 says, "I can do all things through Christ which strengthens me. Notwithstanding ye have done well." Keep moving onward and upward until We are face to face. As you go, remember Phillipians 4:8 says, "Whatsoever things are true, whatsoever things are honest (honorable), whatsoever things are just (right), whatsoever things are pure (holy), whatsoever things are lovely, whatsoever things are of good report (Godly); if there be any virtue and if there be any praise, think on these things. Keep these things in your heart and mind and you are Ever Progressive. You can accomplish all of this because through Christ you can do all things. I AM PROGRESSIVE I AM.

MY THOUGHTS AND NOTES

I AM RICH I AM

In Jeremiah 9:23-24, I say "Let not the rich man glory in his riches." Glory in this that you know and understand ME. Romans 11:33 exclaims, "O the depth of My riches." Ephesians 2:4 says, "I, God, am rich in mercy, because of My great love wherewith I have loved you. According to all of these scriptures mentioned here, I Am rich in mercy, wisdom, knowledge, judgment, and blessings. As Christians we are to tell and teach the non-believers about the unsearchable riches of God in Christ Jesus. God is rich and to seek to understand His riches makes us also rich. As we learn how to be rich in love, patience, understanding, and self-control, we become God's delight. "I Am rich in wisdom and knowledge. My ways are past finding out," because there is such a wealth of ME. I AM RICH I AM.

I AM FAITHFUL I AM

According to II Timothy 2:13, even if you don't believe, I remain faithful, I can not deny myself. Whatever you do I Am the same. If you should fail ME, I Am Faithful still. As a matter of fact, when you fall from grace I pick you up. When you fail in your walk, I forgive and restore you. I Am Faithful. David states that, "I have sworn and will not repent to bless you," (Psalms 110:4). In the beginning I made man, (Genesis 6:5). When I looked around at my creation all I saw was much wickedness. I repented that I had made man. However, I found Noah and his family and saw them as Godly. I Am that spirit that instructed Noah to build (a Safe House), an Ark. Even in this, Noah did not fail Me. He preached as he built the ark. He warned all humanity to repent. I led Noah and his family and caused mated animals to go into the, (Safe House), Ark. I Am who washed the earth down for forty days and forty nights. I had to rid it of the filth and stains and stench of sin, (Genesis 8:21). My child, always remember the day that I repented a second time every time you see a rainbow in the sky. The rainbow is a sign of promise. I promise that I will never totally destroy the earth and flesh again by water in Genesis 9:13.

The flood and the rainbow in the sky were still not enough. After the flood, I needed you to be cleansed, inside also. I wanted to have a real relationship with you as I did in Adam's day. I need to say here that God will not destroy all flesh at once ever again. This He has promised. However the soul that sins shall die, or be cut off from God eternally. This He also promised. Sin is the transgression or the breaking of God's law. Revelation 20:15 says, whosoever is not found written in the book of life, is cast into the lake of fire. This book of life contains the names of those who are filled with the Holy Spirit. Not to have your name in the Book of Life, means that you are separated from God. Spiritually He has no knowledge of you. There is life only in and with GOD. This world will burn with a fervent heat at the end of our days. We must daily examine ourselves to be sure that we are worthy to escape from this world to a place that God has prepared for them that love Him. That place of refuge and safety is heaven. We must live everyday "Rapture Ready."

I am who sent My son, Jesus who hung on a rugged, splinter filled cross. He hung between heaven and earth. The people who did not know who he was, whipped his back and spit in his face. They pierced his hands and feet with the nails that held him to the cross. With a spear, they pierced his side. By Jesus' blood that was spilled and the water that ran from his side, you are washed from your sins today. You are cleansed inside. I Am faithful to keep you clean when you commit to walk in My precepts and to keep my law. I Am faithful and my mercy is renewed for you everyday. I will keep you from failing is what Lamentations 3:23 states about Me. Peradventure you do fall, My son Jesus is the advocate between you and I. My son is holy, but I sent Him to earth in the likeness of sinful flesh. I needed him to be tempted in all things as you are. He was touched with your feelings of infirmity. He knows what it feels like to be tempted by the things of the flesh. Jesus understands your pain and weakness. I Am a spirit and no flesh could look upon nor touch ME. Because I Am a spirit, I could not feel the things of the flesh. Yet, because of Jesus, I will answer when you call. I will comfort when you cry. I will strengthen when you grow weary. Jesus bridged the gulf between us. And He is your advocate that I might know your feelings. I Am Faithful. I Am with you always. After our sons' passing, the only thing I could remember, was the faithfulness of God. His promises are real and because He is truth, I knew He would never leave us nor forsake us. This belief and knowledge held us together. We know that God is that **FAITHFUL I AM.**

I AM TRUTH I AM

Today there is so little of this, My Truth Attribute. However, wherever truth is, I Am. As Christians, we must tell the truth even if it hurts. In Psalms 89:34, God said "My covenant I will not break." In Psalms 89:14, "Justice and judgment are the habitation of My throne and truth is before My face." In other words, truth is the only thing I will rest upon. In John 17:17, my son, Jesus, is praying that you be sanctified through My truth. Today, I Am that truth that you are sanctified by. My throne or habitation is wherever there is truth. Let Me be the one enthroned upon your heart as that Living Truth which is found only in My word. Walk in the light (understanding) of my word and you will never fall, because you walk in truth.

There are many situations and facts that are called truths. For example, the doctors may tell us that we have cancer, heart trouble or whatever. This may be factual according to tests and diagnostic scans. However, the truth is that we do not have to stay this way. The real truth is, by the strips on Jesus' back we were healed. Our finances may be thin to none. Jobs fold, businesses downsize and go high-tech or robotic. We find ourselves needing money for food, shelter and clothing. These are true facts. However, the real truth is that God is our source. We have no need to worry or be anxious, because our Heavenly Father feeds the little birds of the air. Matthew 6:26 asks the question…"Are ye not much better than they?" Why worry "O ye of little faith?" The real truth is, our heavenly father knows that we have need of all these things. The truth is, God's loving favor far exceeds monetary wealth everyday. The truth is that if we seek God first and all of His righteousness, all that we need and most of what we want will be added unto us.

The fact is that we have loved ones addicted to substances that alter their minds and thusly their actions. We feel that jail or death is their ultimate end. The real truth is, God is not willing that anyone should perish. II Peter 3:9 states that, "God is longsuffering (patient) toward us, not willing that any should perish." But He wants all of us to come to a state or place of repentance. Mortal mans facts are, there is no way we can live sinless today. Infidelity, homosexuality, corporate fraud, child abuse, fornication and addictions are a way of life for a lot of people. The real truth is, Jesus died to debunk all of these facts. For infidelity—God is a covenant keeper and he gives us power and shows us how to live true to our mates, even as we are true to our commitment to live holy. Homosexuality is the way of the devil. When we choose to have an appetite for the things that are pure and holy, we will not defile our bodies in such a manner. For corporate fraud—what about the command "thou shall not steal." Maybe that "seems" to be the only way to get ahead today. After all "everybody is doing it." The real truth is "let your yea be yea and your nay, nay." Maintain your integrity. **I, (God), will not let you be tempted or pressed beyond what you are able to endure.** Child abuse is so wide spread, it seems to be an epidemic. Children are God's heritage. Jesus said, "suffer the little children to come unto Me, for of such is the kingdom of heaven." God is watching us. Take care of his heritage or pay the ultimate price of eternal separation from God's presence. Children are the closest to God's heart because of their innocence. Hurt one of His "Little Ones" and you seal your own fate.

The fact and truth is that God created sex. Therefore, sex is a good and beautiful and normal act. The problem comes when we have sex outside of the perimeter that God has set. Unlawful sex of any kind, homosexuality, adultery, or fornication are sins against our own bodies. Except we repent and turn and do it God's way we are sure to reap the harvest of seeds of fire that are sown in our flesh. Sow the seeds of fire and disease, heartbreak, broken homes, and lost loved ones will be our harvest. The real truth is, God, the author and finisher of our faith is well able and will finish the good work that He has planned in you. The real truth is, **by the power of the Holy Spirit. I teach you to walk upright.** Addictions are nothing more than the absence of God in your life. God satisfies like nothing and no one. Walk with God and be free of all filthiness of the flesh. **Walk with me because I AM TRUTH I AM.**

I AM RESCUE I AM

There hath no temptation taken you but such as is common to man: but, I, (God), am faithful, and will not allow you to be tempted or pressed beyond what you are able to bear. Remember in times of temptation, I have already made a way to "escape." In I Corinthians 10:13, I Am that rescue spoken of in the book of Daniel chapter 6. Daniel was thrown into a den of lions. The day after, his non-believing king acknowledged ME and declared that I had rescued Daniel. I deliver and I Am rescue. I allowed Daniel to worship Me even during his captivity. I don't always rescue out of. Daniel 6:27 states… "He delivereth and rescueth, and he worketh signs and wonders in heaven

and in earth…" I take pleasure in rescuing you "out of" but I "go through" with you and make you victorious. When men see you triumph in your trouble My name is glorified because I AM RESCUE I AM.

I AM SHELTER I AM

David in Psalms 61:3 said, "That I had been a shelter for him and a strong tower from his enemy." What he meant in this declaration, is that I Am his personal dwelling place. Also, I was a place to protect him from his enemies. I Am a strong tower and shelter for the righteous. My name is a strong tower. The righteous dwell there and are safe. To paraphrase Joel 3:16, the last part of that verse says, "The heavens and earth will shake when God speaks. But the Lord will be a shelter for his people. Abide in Me. I'll shelter you during your life's stormy situation. I AM SHELTER I AM.

I AM THE DOOR I AM

In Hosea 2:5-6, "Their mother hath played the harlot…she said, I will go after my lovers that give me my bread and my water, my wool and my flax, mine oil and my drink. However, I will hedge up the way with thorns, and make a wall, that she shall not find her paths." I do this because I do not want you to lose your way. Hosea 2:15 encourages…Stay within my door and "…I will give her vineyards from thence, and the valley of Achor for a door of hope." I Am speaking to my prophet about my bride Israel. Israel has tried to go away from Me to live a harlot and worship idol gods. I Am the door for her not to leave Me yet to come back to me after her season of backsliding. I open doors that man can not. I close doors and build hedges of protection for My people. No man can stop Me when I bless. I Am your door of hope, of repentance, and of restoration. I AM your door of opportunity to escape and to protection and safety. I stand at the entrance of the sheepfold and I keep the wolves from My sheep. I also keep My sheep from wandering. David said that My rod (word) and staff (chastisement) were comforting to him. (Psalms 23) I protect in love. I AM THE DOOR I AM.

I AM HOPE I AM

Jeremiah 17:7 records…blessed is the man that trusts in the Lord and whose hope the Lord is. **I Am that Lord of hope. You can speak to yourselves in psalms and hymns and spiritual songs, singing and making melody in your heart unto ME. Give thanks to ME always for all things because I AM your hope. I will not permit you to be made ashamed when you trust and hope in ME. Rejoice in ME, your hope in glory. The world hopes endlessly always, but I Am your endless hope forever. Whenever you need, I Am hope. My children do not despair. My children do not deny that there is a problem in your life. Always know (my children), that I AM in control. Your hope is in ME and you are safe.** David said to Me…thou art my hope…thou art my trust from my youth, (Psalms 71:5). In I Timothy chapter one, Paul acknowledges My Son, Jesus Christ, as your hope. **I Am your hope in glory. Hope in Me until you arrive on heavenly streets. I AM HOPE I AM.**

I AM HEALER I AM

In Exodus 15:26, Moses tells my children for ME that if they would just diligently give ear to my voice and do what is right in My sight and keep all of My commandments they would not suffer the things that the Egyptians (heathen) suffered. I declare that I Am the Lord that healeth thee. Psalms 147:3 says that, "I heal the broken heart and bind up their wounded spirit." In Psalms 103:3, "I forgive all thine iniquities: and heal all thy diseases." I Am the generator of your perpetual health. I heal your sin nature and I heal all your physical diseases. I restore your emotions to wholeness. Turn to ME, I AM the God that healeth thee. It is a continual thing when you are in ME and I in you. Sometimes past habits will cause us to suffer in our bodies. This does not negate the fact that God is our healer. Bitterness, unforgiveness, envy, strife, and hatred, all set our bodies up for the enemy (sickness and even death) to have free reign in us. Let not anger rest in your bosom. Forgive even as you want God to forgive you. Envy will rot your bones. Bitterness is as consumption in our bodies. Purge your minds and hearts and let healing begin. Healing is part of our salvation package. By Jesus' stripes our healing was bought and paid for on Calvary. **Healing is My Children's Bread. I AM HEALER I AM.**

I AM DELIVERANCE I AM

What is it that you need or want my child? Let ME show you what I can do. In Isaiah 43:16, "I make a way in the sea, and a path in the mighty waters." Forget your past and don't consider your old things, (vs.18). I will do a new thing...I will even make a way in the wilderness, and in your dry place, your desert place, I'll make a river, (vs.19). I Am deliverance, look always to ME. I am a very (or ever) present help in the time of your troubles. I deliver you out of them all because, I AM DELIERANCE, I AM.

I AM SAVIOR I AM

"I, even I, am the Lord; and beside me there is no savior," (Isaiah 43:11)..."Before time, before the day was, I Am HE; and there is none that can deliver out of my hand," (Isaiah 43:13). I am your only savior. Some people trust in riches, knowledge, power, and strength...but, I AM Riches, Never Failing, and Salvation. In Colossians, "I have delivered you from the power of darkness. I have planted you into the kingdom of my dear Son." I did this as your savior because, I AM SAVIOR I AM.

I AM RESTORATION I AM

Through my prophet Isaiah (58:12), I Am speaking "and they shall build the old waste places: thou shalt raise up the foundations of many generations: and thou shalt be called, the repairer of the breach, the restorer of paths to dwell in." When you give diligent heed to my word this is what I cause you to do. I Am Restoration of those things that you think are lost to you. When Sarah and Abraham's bodies were old and past the time of reproduction, I restored youth to their bodies. Because of faith in ME, I restored life to their union and they produced Issac. Abraham's faith in My promises was counted as righteousness to him.

We all remember the story or parable of the prodigal son. This parable is in Luke chapter 15 beginning with verse 12. We are so many times like this young man. Being of substantial wealth, health and intelligence, we try to make it on our own. **When I restored the prodigal son to his right thinking, he went**

back to his father. The father said, "Behold here is my son that was once dead, but now is alive." The father then restored him back to family statues or sonship. We must remember that we belong to God and apart from Him we can do nothing. We are dead without God. No matter what the breach when we understand that we are the property of God, He can and He will restore us. The great but wicked King of Babylon, Nebuchadnezzar, was cursed by God. God cursed him because of his self-pride and arrogance. However, God restored King Nebuchadnezzar, but only after he looked to heaven and acknowledged that God reigns supreme in all ways, (Daniel 4). The King was restored to right thinking and to his throne. **I will restore you. I will enable you to repair that broken thing in your life. I also will cause you to restore and repair your path. David declared in Psalms 23:3, that I even restored his soul. In Jeremiah chapter 30 and verse 17, I am talking to Jacob about the restoration of Israel. I said, "I will restore health unto thee, and I will heal thy wounds." I will show mercy where I have in the past chastised you.** God can and does clean the heart and renew the spirit of man. Jesus' death opened the way for us to totally alter our way of thinking and acting. **I AM YOUR RESTORATION I AM.**

I AM COVENANT KEEPER I AM

In Psalms 89:34, I say, **"My Covenant I will not break nor alter the thing that has gone out of my lips." If I said it, it is so. If I promised it, that thing will come to pass. Even if you cannot see and do not understand the how or the wherefore, just believe. Just perceive that It Is, because I have spoken it. I do not have to be in a hurry to bring a promise to pass, because I live forever. I am the God of promise and of patience and of time."** According to II Peter 3:8-9, We are admonished to not be ignorant of this one thing…that one day is with God as a thousand years, and a thousand years as one day. **I am not slack (inept nor weak). I am Marriage Covenant. In the marriage I cause them to have singleness of heart, (Jeremiah 32:39-40). And I will give them one heart, and one way, that they may fear Me forever, for the good of them, and of their children after them: and I will make an everlasting covenant with them, that I will not turn away from them, to do them good; but I will put my fear (reverence) in their hearts, that they shall not depart from Me. I created Adam and Eve and made them husband and wife. It was My pleasure to author the Marriage Covenant. I am Spiritual Covenant through Jesus Christ. I Am the author and finisher of your faith. My covenant with you is a**

Blood Covenant and it is stronger than life. Our covenant is everlasting and endures forever. Spiritually, I fill you with the Holy Ghost and that with power so that you are alive in Me. You will act just like Me. I am the God of Israel that saw you before your time. I swear by My own Holiness and I change not. I AM THE GOD OF COVENANT I AM.

I AM AUTHORITY I AM

I have authorized you in the name of My Son Jesus to do all things. In all that you do, do it in the name or authority of Jesus. By Me you are authorized to cast our devils and proclaim liberty to them that are bound, in the name of Jesus. Under the authority of Jesus' name you can command your way-ward child to be set free from the clutches of satan. Calling on the name of Jesus, cast sickness out of your body. In the name of Jesus command your finances to cover your needs. In the name of Jesus, loose the one addicted to drugs and alcohol. I have given you the authority by the power that is in the name of Jesus to take back that which the enemy (devil) has stolen from you. Take authority and command the blood of Jesus to cover your children and spouses everyday. By the power that is in the name of Jesus, authorize guardian angels to stand guard around all of your properties and vehicles both night and day. In the authority of the name of Jesus you have power to walk upright and to live holy. You have power to abstain from all unrighteousness by the authority that is in the name of Jesus. When My Son arose from the grave, He declared "all power is in My hands." Because we have been adopted into this royal priesthood and are ambassadors for Christ, we are authorized to call the name of Jesus. At the name of Jesus the devil trembles. You have power because by the authority of Jesus name I have given it to you by the Holy Ghost. I have authority over the storms in your life. I speak to the clouds. I ride every wave and I command the winds to cease and be still. In the name of Jesus you have that same authority. I and My son Jesus are one. And you in Jesus, can do all things. I have given authority to you because I AM AUTHORITY I AM.

MY THOUGHTS AND NOTES

I AM SUFFICIENCY I AM

In II Corinthians 3:5-6, my apostle declares that…"we are not sufficient of ourselves" to think anything (self-grandisement) of ourselves. He went farther to say that your sufficiency is of Me, God. I enable and I equip you. I AM the God of the "Blank Check." If there is a need in your life, I already have the solution. I cause you to have those things that suffice your daily needs. I Am sufficiently more to you than I was to your forefathers. For your Fathers, I gave the law which was a type and a shadow of great and wonderful things to come. That thing was (is) the Holy Ghost. Through the Holy Spirit, I Am sufficiently in and with you. I give you sufficient love, faith, grace, and boldness to proclaim life to a dying world. I Am sufficient light in you to light your path way. I Am a lamp to your feet so that you will not error as you walk with Me. I Am your sufficiency for all that is right and holy. Godliness with contentment is great gain because you understand that I AM SUFFIENT I AM.

I AM COMPASSION I AM

Lamentations 3:22 states,…it is because of My mercy that you are not consumed. You see, My compassion fails not. They are renewed every morning, because great is My compassion and faithfulness. My compassion protects you from yourself. I do not hold your faults and failures against you when you seek My face in repentance. In Psalms 86:15, I Am Compassionate friend. David knew Me as, "compassionate and full of grace with mercy." David was a wreck, but he was always after my heart. I showed him My Compassionate love. He said, "Thou O Lord art a God full of Compassion." My child, how do you know Me? I declare unto you I AM COMPASSION I AM.

I AM INVESTMENT I AM

When my spirit is in you, I have equipped you. In Luke 10:7, I send you to minister. I send you to speak peace and to live holy. I Am invested in you by My might and power. Do not be anxious about the faces of the people, the masses, nor the money. Go forth and minister. Just go into my vineyard and work. Where you go, if peace is there, remain there until your mission is accomplished. As you leave, deposit your peace that I have given to you, in that place. I have invested the ministry of peace and of reconciliation in you. Mend the broken hearts. Preach the gospel of peace to them that are bound. Open blinded eyes by the light of my word. This is My time, preach what is the acceptable year of the Lord. My laborers are worthy of their hire. Go and do my will. I pay My kingdom Workers with benefits that are totally out of this world. Be not weary in well doing. If you faint not, you will reap the benefits of your labor in your season. I AM INVESTMENT (in you) I AM.

I AM PROVIDER I AM

I am provision for your life and the life to come. I have a place for you to be with Me and My Son later. I have provided my Spirit so that one day we can all be together at My holy throne. I know what you have need of now though. If I provide for the lilies, the sparrows, and ants, how much more will I provide your needs? By faith, your forefathers received the promise before their deaths. I promised a day of resurrection and a home in heaven. Hebrews 11:40 says, God having provided some better thing for us, that they (forefathers) without us should not be made perfect. I provide a place for the believer and the faithful to escape to after this life. In Exodus 16:35, I provided bread from heaven in the wilderness for the Israelites. I will provide grace for you in your wilderness times also. In John 6:1-12, I provided food for thousands. Through My son, Jesus, I multiplied their provision until all were satisfied. I provided more than enough. There were twelve baskets of leftovers. What do you need in your life? I will provide. I Am the God of more than enough. My power will never diminish, because I AM PROVIDER I AM.

I AM JUST I AM

I Am Just, "but not always Fair," the carnal minded will say. However, I AM "merciful to the unrighteous and I'll remember their sins no more," (Hebrews 8:11-12). I Am in Christ Jesus redeeming you and forgiving your sins. I AM Just even when your walk does not merit My loving justice. I show My loving justice because I know you and I see what I plan for you to become while you are still in your mess. I guide you and hold you and forgive your sins. I am Just and will not cut you off before I Am through making you. I am the author and finisher of your faith. I know the plans that I have for you in ME. I am faithful and just to complete the good work that I have begun in you. II Timothy 2:13 says "if we believe not, yet He abideth faithful." I cannot deny Myself because I AM JUST, I AM.

I AM JUDGMENT I AM

Psalms 25:8-9 explains that because I AM the righteous judge, "I guide My own into the judgment and teach them My way." Romans 11:13 ponders "how unsearchable are my judgments, and my ways are past finding out,"…there is also a Day of Judgment coming. I will be there. I am Just Judgment. I judge the words of your mouth and the meditation of your heart. I know your thoughts afar off. When the words of your mouth line up with My word you will have what you say (or declare). When the meditations of your heart are right I judge you, and your judgment is more righteousness for your walk. Heed my command and encouragement to live holy. Be sure that your deeds line up with all that is right and holy. In My Day of Judgment, all flesh will be judged. Be sure that you live so that you will enter into My rest. I Am the righteous judge in judgment. All will receive a just recompense of reward and I AM not a respecter of persons. You will receive for the good that you have done. You will also be punished for unforgiven sins. All unholy deeds of the flesh that are not cleansed by Jesus' blood will come forth in My Day of Judgment. I am righteous to reward all for his or her deeds. I make no mistakes. Be sure that your sins are washed away and covered by the cleansing blood of Jesus. I will not forget the good that you have done because…I AM YOUR JUDGMENT I AM.

I AM MERCY I AM

I, Mercy, "rejoice against judgment," (James 2:13). It is not my nature to punish you. You are made in my image and my likeness. It pleases Me when your transgressions are covered by My love and mercy. I rejoice when I can not judge you because of my mercifulness. In the book of Micah chapter 6 verse 8, the writer spells out what I require of you. I require that you "do

justly and love mercy." Matthew 5:7 reminds us that the "merciful are blessed." When we show forth mercy, God is just to show us mercy when we really deserve judgment. To have mercy and to show mercy makes one happy in his heart. Proverbs 3:3 admonishes us to "not let mercy and truth forsake us." **Hold onto my mercy attribute and you will find favor in My sight and in the eyes of your fellowman. Psalms 85:10 says, "mercy and truth are met together and righteousness and peace have kissed each other." When you walk in love and peace, My mercy and grace will sustain you.** Our righteousness is as filthy rags and amounts to nothing when we do our alms without a heart of mercy. Our tithes and free will offerings and volunteer work, make us appear before God as hypocrites when we do not show mercy. The main things we should focus on in service for God are judgment (mostly for ourselves) mercy (always for others) and faith in God. God says to us, **"I Am ever full of Mercy"** because I AM MERCY I AM.

I AM TEACHER I AM

James 1:5 states, "if any of you lack wisdom just ask Me, God. I give to all men liberally." I will not fuss at you. I will never tire of your asking. I will not call you stupid. I will never ask, "what you did with the last dose of wisdom that I have already given you?" I will just give you more wisdom so that you will know My way. Proverbs 9:9 makes this observation—"give instruction to a wise man, and he will be yet wiser: teach a just man an he will increase in learning." My word is your School Master. I have even given to you how to deal with My heritage. Train up a child in the way he/she should go. Teach them about Me as I, through My Son and the Prophets and Apostles have taught you. Teach your children so that My ways will not depart from their memory when they are mature in age. Teach them about Me and they will be wise in their walk with ME. Teach by your words and through your actions.

My desire and plan for you is that you are ahead only and not trailing behind. I teach you how to have an excellent spirit and a perfect walk. Hosea 4:6 says that, "My people are destroyed for lack of knowledge." I am not willing that any one perish or suffer lack. We as Christians must not reject the word of wisdom or knowledge coming from Gods anointed ones. They are anointed to teach us the ways of God. **I Am the great teacher. Take time to learn of Me. I AM (never retiring) TEACHER I AM.**

I AM WISDOM I AM

The actual beginning of wisdom in you is your fear (or reverence) of Me. According to Psalms 111:10, Solomon was an upright man in the sight of God. When God asked Him how could he further bless him,…"**Just what more can I do for you Solomon?**" Solomon answered God by asking Him to show him how to walk among and minister to His people. He said, "show me how to go in and out (to walk) among your people." Because of his heart, God did exceeding and abundantly more than he had asked. When we seek the wisdom of God, he gives us wisdom and exceeding understanding. In I Kings 4:19-31, "God gave Solomon (even) largeness of heart," meaning he expanded Solomon's love-walk. Solomon's wisdom excelled the wisdom of all. He was wiser than all men; his fame was in all nations round about." If you want to be famous—just hook up with God. Proverbs 4:5, instructs us to "get wisdom and get understanding." Talk about the wisdom of God and do not let His words cease from your mouth. Proverbs 4:7 says, **I, Wisdom, am the principle thing. Therefore, seek My attribute of wisdom. It will exhault you and promote you in all ways.** Wisdom keeps us in the right way. **James 1:5 instructs, if you lack wisdom…if you are at all deficient here…ask ME. I give to all men liberally and do not recount or record your weakness. In James 3:17, "My wisdom that comes from Me is pure, peaceable, gentle, easy to receive and exchange, full of mercy and good fruits." I Am no respecter of persons. I AM not "two-faced" when I endow with My wisdom. Seek wisdom of Me because I AM (that) WISDOM I AM.**

I AM HONOR I AM

Live and walk in honor as you, above all else, guard your heart with all diligence. What comes out of us is who we are. Out of our hearts comes the issues of life, (Proverbs 4:23). We must be sure that what we do mirrors God's attribute of honor. Always check your motives. Do they line up with God's will or are we trying to impress someone else to get ahead. Also we are "snared by the words of our mouths," (Proverbs 6:2). You must let the words of your mouth always honor

God. In business, in pleasure, in worship, in everyday life our words have to be acceptable unto God. Be careful that we always speak and declare the words of our God of Honor. In Psalms 91:1, "when we remain in God's presence (secret place) we abide under this protective "shadow of the almighty." As found in verse 9 and 10 of Psalms 91, God causes us to walk in honor, because we make Him our lifestyle. Everyday and in every way all praises go to the only true, wise and invisible God our father. We give Him glory and honor forever when we worship Him and obey His word. This honor to God continues generation after generation, because God is Honor. Honor God as you abide always under the shadow of this almighty protection and He will give you honor. **Let Honor be your way of life, because I AM HONOR I AM.**

I AM FRIEND I AM

I AM Friend to those who are not ashamed to call ME "Friend." Because of his faith and righteousness I called Abraham "My friend." I do not judge by your looks or your clothing or ethnicity as to whether or not you can be my friend. In James 2:2-4, the saints were admonished not to have respect of person, because of ones apparel. God does not choose us by how well we look. We are mainly chosen because our hearts are a mess. Our lives are ragged and we stink like sin, this draws God to us. These are the people that God will readily befriend. Proverbs 17, and the first part of verse 17, says that "A friend loveth at all times." It does not matter whether or not you are rich, fair to look at nor popular. A friend loves "just because." There is a criteria for God's friendship though. God will not "bowl us over" to be in relationship with us. Even in the natural, a man that has friends must first show himself friendly. Also, we have a friend "that sticketh closer than a brother" in Proverbs 18:24. A friend is careful how they treat other friends. Song of Solomon 5:16 states,…"his mouth is sweet…this is my beloved and this is my friend"…We as Christians should be best friends of the Cause of the Christ. Always declaring the sweetness of God's word and will. John 15:13-15, talks about us…"Greater love hath no man than this, that a man lay down his life for his friend." Jesus gave all for us (His life). **I, God, sacrificed my Son just so I can be your friend. As my friend, I need you to be able to act in a certain way. This you could not do without the shed blood of My son Jesus. His blood covered and cleansed you. John 15:14 says, "you are my friends, if you do whatsoever I command you. Because of Jesus you are no longer called servants, but I call you friend. I AM (your) FRIEND I AM.**

MY THOUGHTS AND NOTES

I AM LIVING WATER I AM

In Me, you are like a watered garden. You are always alive with beauty. You are fragrant and fruitful. I Am a well of water and because of Me…"with joy shall ye draw water" from the wells of water springing out of you. In Matthew 3, you are also buried in water through baptism. This brings you into right standing or a clean conscience toward Me.

In John 4:14, My son Jesus is at a well talking to a sinner who is much like some of you were. He tells her, "whosoever drinketh of this water shall thirst again…" This is natural water from a natural well or spring. Jesus goes on to add, "The water I shall give you shall be in you a well of water springing up into everlasting life." This water, that I through My son, will give you, will sanctify and cleanse through the washing of My word. In Psalms 23:2, not only do I supply water, but in times of trouble I will lead you by stilled waters. I calm the seas and waves of turbulence in your life. I do not stop the water because in it there is life. Because I called forth the waters, I control them. I still your waters. As the living water I Am a fountain in your life's garden. I AM a well of living water. I AM as a spring whose water flow fails not. I AM (the) LIVING WATER I AM.

I AM ABUNDANCE I AM

All of my attributes, I share and impart abundantly. Glorify Me as your abundance. When you think or feel that you have it all, just remember that there is still more of Me. Right now, in your frail human existence, you can only see and know in part. However, there is coming a day (real soon) when partial knowledge and understanding of Me will be done away with and you will behold My glory in its fullest. Even then it will take an eternity to know all. In Ephesians 3:20, I AM He that is able to do Exceeding and Abundantly more above all that you can ever ask or think. You will glorify Me as your abundance, when you make Me abundantly yours.

Job 5:9 accounts that I do "unsearchable and marvelous things without numbers." You cannot count the ways that I bless you. How many times have I supplied your needs? Where are the doors that I opened for you? Count them. You cannot measure my abundance. I bless beyond measure. I have things in store for you that you have not even imagined yet. I measure and I give to everyone according to his or her needs. Need more grace? I have it and it is yours. Do you need healing, financial stability, holy boldness? It is all within My power to give unto you. You only need to let your requests be made known unto ME. Of course, I already know your needs. All I want is for you to acknowledge that your blessings come from My Storehouse of Abundance. In Genesis chapter one, I spoke and things came to pass. I spoke great lights into the elements. I spoke and the waters brought forth abundantly. I spoke and the air abundantly yielded every winged fowl…and it was (all) good. I blessed all of my creation and charged them to be fruitful (abundant) in reproduction of their kind. In the book of Matthew chapter 13, My son Jesus is speaking and He tells His followers "It is given to them to know the mysteries of the kingdom of Heaven." What Jesus' followers were endowed with (power and wisdom) would be given by Me abundantly. 1 Timothy 1:14 says, "The grace of our Lord was exceeding abundant with faith and love which is in Christ Jesus." Look to me for all things. I AM ABUNDANCE I AM.

I AM SOVEREIGN I AM

When it is all said and done…When you take time to meditate on and ponder My ways…When you talk about Me to others, just remember that I Am Sovereign. Whatever you need I Am that. I rule supreme and I reign forever. I will never run out of love, blessing, mercy, wisdom, grace, or provision for you. "You are the reason that I do things. You are the things that I do." I get pleasure from prospering you. You are my righteousness. You are my priests and lords. You are made in My similitude and My likeness. No one can question or judge Me. No one can rightly accuse Me. I Am Sovereign. I reign forever and ever. I do as I please. My pleasure is established in the holy bible. I will accomplish what I desire. "Know therefore this day, and consider it in your heart, that I Am God in heaven above and upon the earth beneath." I Am God in your good times, I Am God in your bad and sad times. I Am God on your mountain tops. Yes I win your battles victoriously. I Am still God in your valley. I show up and show out in your valley experiences. I win all times for you because I Am Sovereign. I Am God when things are right and sunny. I Am your God when it seems the host of hell has come to your dwelling. There is no other God like Me. And Deuteronomy 4:39, testifies of this. I Samuel 2:8 says, "I am the God that created heaven. I created the pillars under heaven and I keep the earth balanced on them." I Am abundantly sovereign. I Am God and the same yesterday, today, and forever. Yes I Am the sovereign ever reigning King. There will never be an end of my throne. My kingdom is established forever. Today I am yet seeking for them that will worship Me and crown Me "King" of their life. I Am Sovereign and there is none like Me.

I Am Alpha and Omega—"I Am the beginning and the end. I Am which is, which was and which is to come," in Revelation 1:8. According to the 38th chapter of Job, I set the ordinances of heaven. I have dominion over planet earth. I tell the waves of the mighty waters how far to come ashore and they obey. The winds obey my voice. I Am the Almighty. Call Me marvelous. My exploits deserve a marvelous expression. I Am everything between A and Z. If you think or need to have it I can be there for you to bless in or out of it. There is no new day or time or era with Me. Things change always with men, but I already know what will happen. I know the end as I am creating the beginning. From everlasting to everlasting I AM…

I Am Omnipotent—the almighty that reigneth supreme. I Am from everlasting to everlasting. I AM outside of the boundaries of time and space. I live forever and of My power there SHALL be NO end.

I Am Omniscient—the all wise and all knowledgeable one. I foreknow. At the beginning I see the end. I created man and his world. I knew that they would fall from their lofty place of communion with Me. I prepared a Savior for fallen man. I created the heaven for them who will embrace this Savior as Lord.

I Am Omnipresent—I Am in every place always watching over you and protecting you. I Am leading and saving you.

I Am Jehovah—I alone am Jehovah. I am Jehovah, Lord of your strength. I am Jehovah over all of your things and stuff. I Am all and total satisfaction guaranteed. I am Jehovah, Lord everlasting. You need not worry about the storms of life. Don't fear life's winds of destruction. Where there seems to be no bridge over your troubled waters—fear not. Right where you need a pathway and when you need a bridge to cross over, I will lay Me down. Let Me take you to the blessed hope that is within you, to that hope that is on the other side of your troubled waters.

I Am Immutable—the never changing redeemer. I swear by my own righteousness. I change not. I'll never vary. I Am not capable nor susceptible to vary from My word. What I say is established forever. Before My word fails heaven and earth will pass away.

Call Me the **Tree of Life** because I AM. In Me you will live forever. I reign forever. I AM alive forever.

Call ME **Hallowed**—I Am Holy without measure. I Am righteous beyond comprehension I AM mighty without failure.

Call ME **Wonderful**—I Am so wonderful that mortal man can only say AWESOME when he speaks regarding Me.

Call ME **Excellent**—I excel in all that I do. My ways are past finding out. My excellence passes all understanding of man.

Call ME **Jehovah Rapha**—I Am always your healer, your constant and perpetual health and well being.

Call ME **Jehovah Shama**—I Am gladly your Hero. I Am always with you. I keep, I save, I help, and I redeem you. **I AM SHAMA I AM.**

Call Me **Jehovah Jireh**—"My provider" is what Abraham said about Me to Isaac. Don't fear the famine situations in your life. My coffers are full and My grain baskets are running over. I Provide the ram in your thicket of tests and trials. I cause you to graze in green pastures and beside still water in spite of and in the middle of the times of famine. Find this recorded about ME in Psalms 23.

Call ME **Jehovah Nissi**—Because I Am your warrior, I Am your whole Army. I alone AM more power with you than the whole of creation is against you. I AM protection. I will hide you in my word until the storms of life are passed. I stand for you until your battle is won. This is so that you can see My glory. I Am Jehovah Nissi, I AM. In Exodus 17:15-16, I do battle for you. You don't have to fight, because the battle is not yours to begin with. Only the victory is yours. The war is mine and I always win for you.

Call Me **Jehovah Shalom**—I AM your Peace, peace that talks to you. In Judges 6:24, Gideon talks about ME. He was perplexed because of the enemy. I sent an angel to speak with him. I AM Shalom I AM. In times of perplexity and helpless feelings I AM Peace…Peace, Perfect Peace. Shalom with nothing missing and nothing broken and no shortages.

Call ME "the **Rose of Sharon.**" I AM fairer than ten thousand. My fragrance blesses without the pain of thorns. I add blessings without sorrow and without pain. I Am sweeter than honey. I AM more precious than gold. Try ME and taste of My goodness. I Am beautiful beyond comprehension.

In weakness I Am **Strength**. I Am waiting to hear you cry "Abba Father." I AM that father that desires to bless you with all good and perfect gifts. If your "desired thing" does not exist, I will create it for you. Try Me. Ask Me to create in you a clean heart and to renew a right spirit within you. I'll do just that. After you have been strengthened, go and strengthen your brother.

I AM that **Hedge of Protection** about you that satan was witness to in Job's day, I AM. I hide you in My word and under My wings, I protect you. I, even I Am He and there is no god beside Me. I make alive and I wound. There is none to stop My hand. I protect them that are mine. I know that you are mine by the way you obey My commandments and by the way you love each other.

I Am the "mind boggling" **Mathematician.** I say give Me your 10% and watch Me multiply your 90% that is left. I cause you to reap the reward of the whole 100%. Because, you see, a little is much when you place it in My hands. Not only do I multiply the substance of your hands, but I'll multiply your years. I multiply the seed of your loins and the fruit of the womb. When you walk in wisdom and in My way, your days shall be "multiplied" and made good: The "years of your life shall be increased" as in Proverbs 9:11. Be faithful in service and in your worship of Me. I multiply and I increase. Remember this—little prayer and you'll have little power. Much prayer, and you have dynamite, earth shaking power. Give it to Me and I will multiply you and yours.

I Am the ultimate **Choreographer** of the dance—I write the songs that sustain you in your midnight season. When the music stops, that is when you will sing your song. God is saying, "I AM your song in the cloudy day. I AM your song in your wilderness. I AM your song that gives life to the dry bones in your valley so that they rise and dance. I AM the sweet melody in your soul. I make even the "lead footed" to float across the floor of a room, with a new dance. Just as David danced before ME, so will I cause your spirit to dance. Dance and rejoice until your spirit has shaken off everything that is not like Me. Let Me create a new song in you. Meditate on ME and I'll keep you singing in your heart. God wants you to keep your song in you. It is where God dwells. Your song is a consecration to God's service. Keep your song as David did and nothing can harm nor offend you. Your song is the praise and worship that you give God daily. Isaiah 61:3 says, put on "the garment of praise for the spirit of heaviness" and I say "sing and dance unto the Lord."

I AM the great **Poet**—I create the happy lyrics to your (would be) sad song. I cause your song to be a melody of praise, worship and adoration for ME. Just open your mouth and watch ME fill it with praise and thanksgiving. The poems of love that are hidden in you, I gave them to you. Praise Me with your heartfelt poetry of love. Let your lips Praise Me with poems of love.

Call ME **Abba Father**—because I AM. I have adopted you into MY kingdom through My spirit. I know who you are when you cry Abba Father, because you are mine. My ear is ever turned to your voice. You are My heritage in My image and My likeness. Yes, I recognize you wherever you are because you are My child. As in the natural…you look like and act like your earthly father, so in the spiritual you shall look and act like ME. In the natural, usually every mother knows her baby's cry. That same mother understands the nature and voice of that cry. That mother knows how to satisfy that crying baby. I, your Heavenly Father, am even more tuned to you. My arms are never heavy. I never sleep or doze. I will always hear and answer My dear children. **I AM your Father.**

I AM the greatest of **Artists**. With just a stroke of my breath; I will turn your dark skies sunny. I color the sky blue. I put the black in the cloud. I green the grass and I red the roses. I beautify even you as you walk with ME in meekness. I create the clean heart. I renew the right spirit in you. I purge those hands that are raised to me. I paint you with favor and loving kindness. **I AM the Artist.**

I AM **Dunamis**—A world changing power I AM. I Am moved through your obedience to My Holy Word. If things don't look right for you, I can turn your world upside down to make it right. I AM world shaping power. I will explode that perfect thing in you. I AM magnified when you yield to ME. I, through My Holy Spirit am power in you. And again in Exodus 3:13-14, when Moses asked ME, "What shall I tell them to call you? What is you name?" I said then and I say even to you today, **"I AM that I AM."**

What do you need? What do you want? Where are you weak? Do you fall short in anything? What is lacking in your life? If there is any need in your life, I will fill it. I AM your everlasting everything...**I AM that I AM.**

MY THOUGHTS AND NOTES

CONCLUSION

After I finished writing this book and was ready to have it typed and edited, I prayed over it. Again our God began to talk. He spoke of a time for **refreshing and revival**. The Lord made me to know that I had to go on. Basically He pressed me to move on with His blessing. One night I had a dream that was so very real to me, and in that dream I heard God say, **"I AM faithful. I will hold you up."**

Well, here we are one year and one month later. Our son James has been gone for a whole year. The time has really flown by. We have gone through many "firsts." Our first Mother's Day, Father's Day, Easter Sunday, Fourth of July, and his first date of birth without him. Thanksgiving, Christmas Eve, and New Year's Day of 2003 were our first without James II. The worst first was the first anniversary of his passing. His wife saw a first Wedding Anniversary without him. Our other two sons watched the first Super Bowl without arguing with their older brother. Our new pastor had a first child in the middle of their transition. He did the first Back To School Sunday with prayer for our young members. Guess what, my faithful readers, by God's grace and mercy, **WE MADE IT!!!!**

For over a week leading up to January 30th, we were receiving phone calls, cards and letters from family and friends far and near. Today is February 8, 2004 and yesterday we received two long distance telephone calls from loved ones telling us that we are yet in their prayers.

For me, some days seem to just drag by. Some days my spirit soars like the mighty eagle. Sometimes the tears come, because of small insignificant things (to others), but these things are precious memories of our dear son, James Edward Striggles II.

Christmas and New Years of 2002 all of our children were with us. Alisa, Rebecca, and I sat and listened to James Sr., James II, Anthony, and Algie tell of their youthful antics and how they survived "parental-floggings." They kept us laughing about church people and some of the funny things that can happen during a church service. Our god-sons, Earl Orr, and Michael Staten were in our home adding their voices to the merriment.

Needless to say, without voicing it, we were all dreading the holidays of 2003. However we try, there is just no way that we can out-think nor out-plan God. On December 8, 2003, our only daughter Rebecca and her high school sweetheart took her dad and I out for dinner. After the meal was over David (very nervously, I might add) asked our permission and blessing for he and Rebecca to marry. On Christmas Eve, at our traditional family dinner, David and Rebecca were officially engaged. They set the wedding date for October 2, 2004. The chair at the dinner table where James II would have been seated was not vacant. There at our table sat a shiny faced, smiling, slightly nervous young man. We all love David Smith and we thank God for him becoming a part of our family. We lost our birth son, but God did not leave us nor forget about us. We had a very joyous holiday season. Also, Alisa (bless her heart) has accepted the awesome task of directing Rebecca's wedding. God is yet faithful to His promise to be with us always even until the end. This is not the end.

Growing up in the church, if I heard it once I've heard it thousands of times, "Come unto me, all ye that labour and are heavy laden, and I will give you rest." (Matthew 11:28) Since January 30, 2003, I have gradually come to really understand and to take heed to Jesus' teaching here. Of course, I always felt (in the back of my mind) that this was Jesus talking to sinners. Oooo Weee!!! Did you know that we can be so ladened with the cares and disappointments of this life that we feel almost hopeless. We so often labour under the load of pain and trouble that our enemy, the devil, thrusts upon us. Until we can hear the voice of our Heavenly Father, calling, "Come, Come, Come unto Me All…" we will remain under that load. Keep in mind that God cares for you. He already knows your end before your beginning. In the middle of your existence, He has sent an advocate and intercessor for us. Our end should always be better than the beginning or the middle now that we are familiar with God and what He wants for us.

There have been days of fear, anxiety, depression, and sadness for us all. I had anxiety attacks when either of my other two sons slept too long. Panic gripped my heart if I would hear Rebecca's alarm clock sound and she did not respond. If my husband slept too deep, I found myself checking to be sure that his heart was still beating. We have a little cousin named Louis Edmondson III that we have been helping to raise. If I go into his room and he has not turned over for a few hours, I find myself flipping the switch of the over-head light. My husband and I run a small daycare. One day a little girl in our care slept for hours. After she had been asleep for two and a half hours, I tried making noise to wake her. She would not even open her eyes. I even turned her over. I then called her mother's job. The long nap was totally out of character for one and a half year old Jordan. I began baby-sitting Jordan when she was barely four weeks old. I knew her habits and daily eating and sleeping routine. Her mother thought it very sweet of me to call her about her daughter. I was relieved that my anxiety was not apparent to my client at the other end of the telephone. Now that she has turned two, occasionally I wish that Jordan and a couple of her playmates would sleep for three to four hours.

There are days that I am afraid to talk to anyone about my feelings that go back and forth. I fear that they will think I am crazy. Where do I go? Who can I turn to? Who will hear and understand what I feel? There is no one but Jesus. Matthew 11:28 is so real to me today. When you have no place to go and no one to talk to, I am reminded that my best friend Jesus himself bids me to come unto Him, because He understands all. It could not have been pleasant for Him in the Garden of Gethesemane. Jesus looked at the cross and saw how much peace and comfort our family would need. He remembered in the book of Isaiah, that the chastisement of my peace would be placed upon Him. He looked again and saw my heart and my plight in this life and He had mercy on me. I can never know the real cost of my deliverance from sin. While on the cross, Jesus cried out to God—"why have you forsaken me?" (Matthew 7:46). He had asked God over and over to relieve him of the task that was before him. He, like us, was heavy ladened with our sins, pains, and sorrows. Once Jesus yielded to the will of God, he was able to go through. My sins were nailed to that cross that held Him. Remember always that the will of God will never take us where His grace and mercy can not sustain us.

And again is there a need in your life? What are you lacking? Take your burdens, your needs, or your lacks to our Father. Whatever you need, God is the solution. He said to Moses, and He yet is saying, **I AM THAT...I AM.**

MY THOUGHTS AND NOTES

I thank God for all of those who prayed for me, and spoke words of encouragement to me as I wrote this book.

I praise and thank My God always, because He alone causes me to triumph in all that I do for Him.

The Author

0-595-33865-8

Printed in the United States
85650LV00005B/403-498/A

9 780595 338658